CHRISTMAS JAZZIN' ABOUT

classic Christmas hits for violin & piano

PAMELA WEDGWOOD

(with special thanks to Charles Knights)

VIOLIN PART

Santa Claus Is Comin' To Town
© 1934 EMI Catalogue Partnership/EMI Feist Catalog Inc., USA
Worldwide print rights controlled by Warner Bros. Publications Inc./IMP Ltd

The Christmas Song
© 1944 Mesquite Music Corp. USA
Warner Chappell Music Ltd, London W1Y 3FA
Used by permission of International Music Publications Ltd

All other titles © 1996 by Faber Music Ltd
First published in 1996 by Faber Music Ltd
3 Queen Square London WC1N 3AU
Music processed by Wessex Music Services
Printed in England by Halstan & Co Ltd

ISBN 0-571-51694-7

To buy Faber Music publications or to find out about the full range of titles available
please contact your music local retailer or Faber Music sales enquiries:
Tel: +44 (0)1279 82 89 82   Fax: +44 (0)1279 82 89 83
Email: sales@fabermusic.com   www.fabermusic.com

FABER ƒƒ MUSIC

Santa Claus Is Comin' To Town

Words by Haven Gillespie
Music by J. Fred Coots

3

Deck the Halls

Ding-Dong-Doodle

O Little Swinging Town of Bethlehem

Wassailing-By!

8

Christmas Jingle

Once in Royal David's City

The Christmas Song
(Chestnuts roasting on an open fire)

Words and Music by
Mel Tormé and Robert Wells

Past Three o'Clock

CHRISTMAS JAZZIN' ABOUT

classic Christmas hits for violin & piano

PAMELA WEDGWOOD

(with special thanks to Charles Knights)

CONTENTS

Santa Claus is Comin' to Town
© 1934 EMI Catalogue Partnership/EMI Feist Catalog Inc., USA
Worldwide print rights controlled by Warner Bros. Publications Inc./IMP Ltd

The Christmas Song
© 1944 Mesquite Music Corp. USA
Warner Chappell Music Ltd, London W1Y 3FA
Used by permission of International Music Publications Ltd

All other titles © 1996 by Faber Music Ltd
First Published in 1996 by Faber Music Ltd
3 Queen Square London WC1N 3AU
Music processed by Wessex Music Services
Printed in England by Halstan & Co Ltd

ISBN 0 571 51694 7

FABER *ff* MUSIC

2

Santa Claus Is Comin' To Town

Words by Haven Gillespie
Music by J. Fred Coots

With a good swing

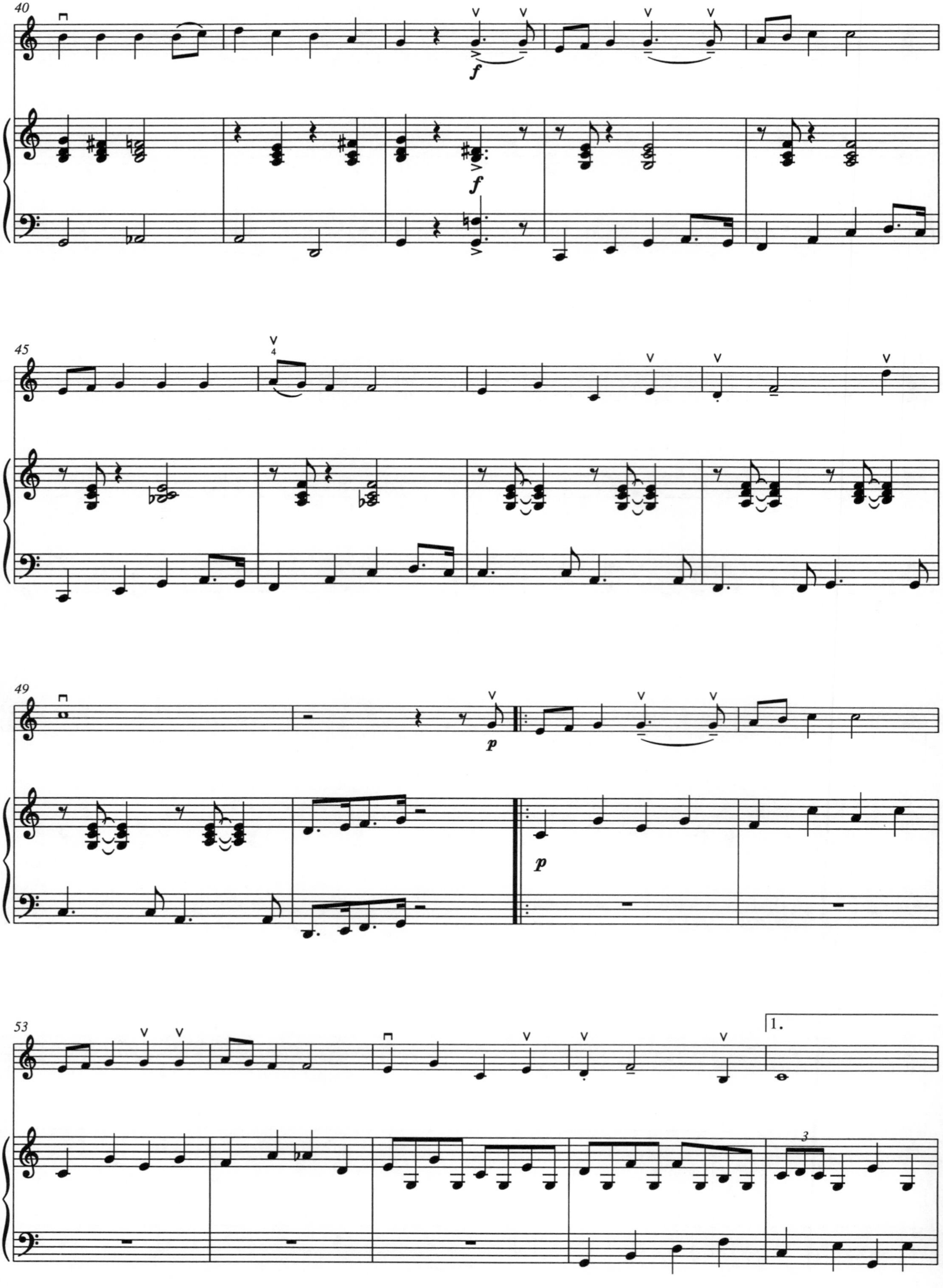

40
f
f
45
4
49
p
p
53
1.
3

Deck the Halls

8

Ding-Dong-Doodle

O Little Swinging Town of Bethlehem

12

Wassailing-By!

with a good swing!

Christmas Jingle

Slowly (♩ = 96)

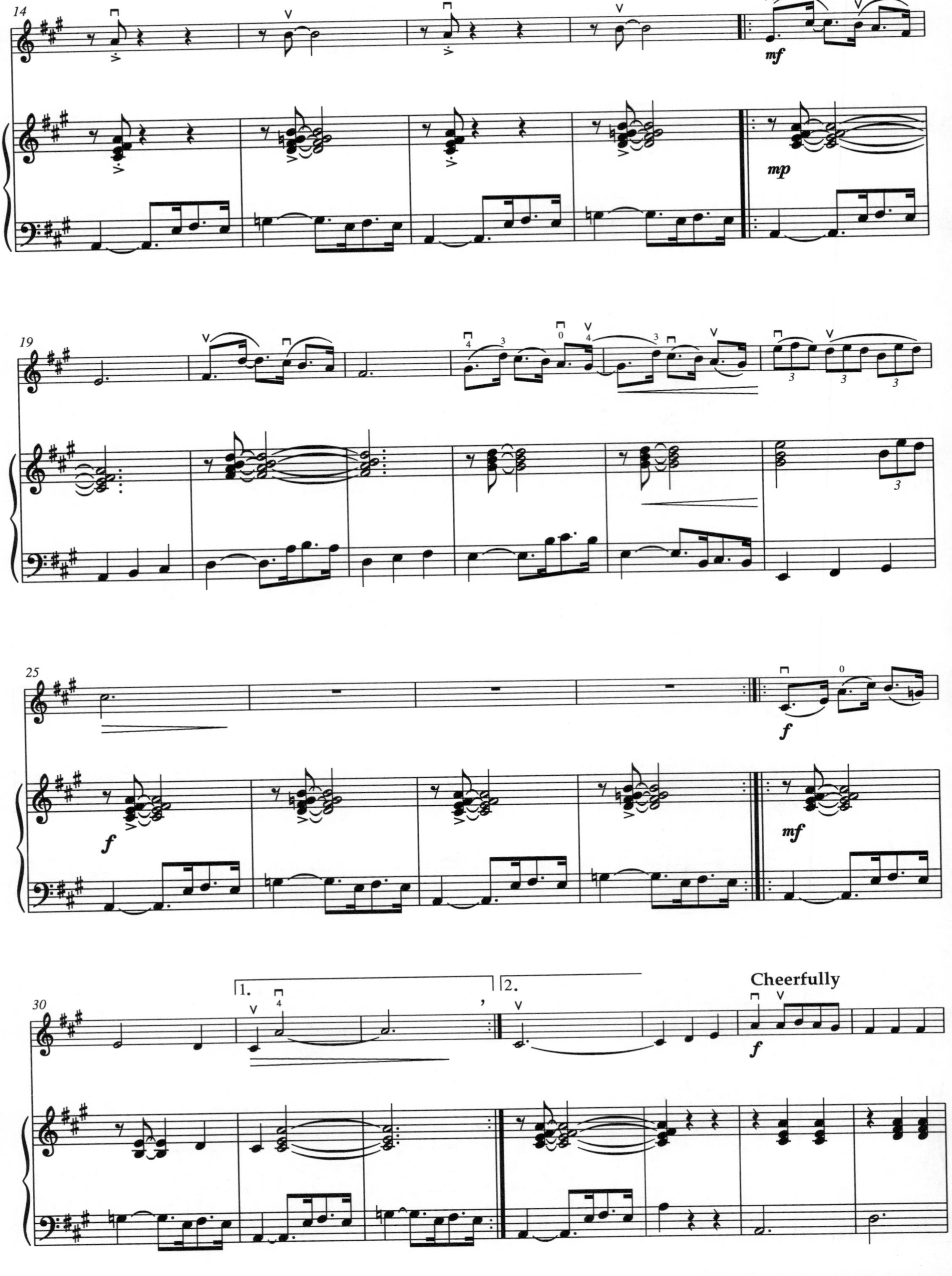
mf
mp
f
mf
1.
2.
Cheerfully
f

Once in Royal David's City

Majestically (♩ = 76)

The Christmas Song
(Chestnuts roasting on an open fire)

Words and Music by
Mel Tormé and Robert Wells

Relaxed (♩ = 80)

22

Past Three o'Clock

24

MALLARD PRESS

An imprint of BDD Promotional Books Company, Inc.,
666 Fifth Avenue, New York, N.Y. 10103

Mallard Press and its accompanying design and logo
are trademarks of BDD Promotional Book Company, Inc.

CLB 2341
Copyright © 1990 Colour Library Books Ltd.,
Godalming, Surrey, England.
Copyright © 1990 Illustrations: Oxford Scientific Films Ltd.,
Long Hanborough, England.
First published in the United States of America
in 1990 by The Mallard Press
Printed and bound in Italy by Fratelli Spada, SpA
All rights reserved.
ISBN 0 792 45034 5

· Oxford Scientific Films ·

CATS

Michael Leach

MALLARD
PRESS

Contents

*Previous page: a black-footed cat. Left: an
Indian tiger, safe from poachers within the
boundaries of Ranthambhore National Park.*

1
What is a Cat?

Cats are probably the most efficient hunters in the animal kingdom. They are silent, fast and well-armed; perfectly adapted for killing *prey*. Being at the top of many food chains, they have few predators other than man. The cat family is also widespread, and members of it can be found almost everywhere in the world except Australia and the polar regions. There are thirty-five known *species* and no matter what their size, from the tiny sand cat of North Africa to the huge Siberian tiger, they are all basically similar. Moreover, with the exception of the male lion, which has a thick mane, both sexes usually look alike. But male cats are usually bigger and heavier than the females, and they are often slower as a consequence of their extra weight.

A cat's sense of smell is not as good as a dog's, but they do have excellent hearing and good eyesight. In darkness, cats can also use their long, sensitive whiskers to "feel" their way around. However, even after all these senses have been used to locate the prey, the cat still has to catch it. Cats are not good at running long distances, but they are very fast over short ones. Their long, powerful legs give them amazing acceleration in quick bursts.

Cats run on soft, fleshy pads which are deeply marked; the marks act like the treads on a car tire, giving extra grip. The pads also serve as cushions, making the cat's movements almost impossible to hear. Its claws, the cat's most deadly weapons, are sheathed inside these paw pads. Apart from the cheetah and the strange, flat-headed cat, most cats have claws that can be tucked away inside their paws when they are not needed. When a cat attacks, its claws are sprung out by strong muscles and immediately the cat is armed with razor-sharp hooks that are wickedly curved to help them hold onto struggling prey. They have five claws on each front paw and four on each of the back ones.

Claws are not, of course, the only weapon in the cats' armory: their teeth are extremely well-adapted for catching and eating. For example,

the four long, sharp *canine* teeth – two on the top and two on the bottom jaw – are used for killing prey and tearing meat. But perhaps the strangest speciality of a cat is its rasp-like tongue. It is so rough that it can lick meat right off the bone. Even a small cat's tongue feels like sandpaper, but were a lion to lick your skin, it would tear off and disappear in seconds.

There are seven species of big cats and twenty-eight species of small cats, but it is not only size that differentiates them. For instance, big cats can roar but cannot purr, and small cats cannot roar but can purr. A big cat rests with its front feet stretched out in front of its body, whereas a small cat relaxes with its front paws tucked neatly under its chest. The other main difference between them is that small cats crouch down when they feed while big cats eat lying down.

Above: an Indian tiger. This animal's forward-facing eyes, in common with those of other cats, help it to judge distance accurately. The thick mane of the male lion (facing page) makes it look bigger and stronger than it really is.

2
Life Among the Cats

On the whole, cats do not get along well with other cats. Lions are the only species that spend much of their lives together in a group. Sometimes cheetahs will join together in a loose pack for short periods, but all the other cats are solitary hunters that defend their *territory* against all rivals, feline and non-feline.

Male cats usually have much larger territories than females, and within one male's range there might be two or three females. A male cat will tolerate the presence of females in his territory, although he will have nothing to do with them until the breeding season. But if another male should cross his border, he will drive him off.

Like all wild animals, cats try to solve their territorial disputes without fighting and initially warn intruders not to come too close. For example, tigers roar every few minutes when they are near the edge of their territory, and jaguars give out short, rough grunts which can be heard from up to two miles away. In addition, males mark their boundaries unmistakably with a sprayed mixture of urine and a strong-smelling liquid from a special *scent gland*. This scent tells other males that the area is already occupied.

If rival cats do meet there is a lot of noise but usually very little action. They hiss and spit and cause their hair to stand on end to make themselves look bigger. Such bluffing can carry on for up to half an hour before one of the cats loses heart and retreats. This behavior is intended to stop either cat being hurt in a fight: a relatively slight injury may prevent them from hunting effectively and, in such a case, the cat might die

The Canadian lynx is a nocturnal hunter that preys on rodents, birds and small deer.

Completely at home in water, the fishing cat of Asia catches fish by scooping them up with its paw.

Its high vantage point on a tree stump allows this lynx to look around for prey or signs of danger.

hunters usually have uniformly brown coats without stripes or other markings. The lynx of Europe and North America starts to hunt just before sunset, and its yellow/brown fur makes it almost invisible in the glow of the sinking sun.

of starvation as a consequence of the wounds rather than from the wounds themselves.

Most cats are *nocturnal*; their silent paws and eyes specially suited to low light are perfectly adapted to hunting during the night. A few cats, such as the cheetah and jungle cat, do hunt in daylight, but most cats would rather hunt in the cooler temperatures of the night. A small number of cats become active at dusk and dawn, when there is still enough light to see well but it is not too hot to run and catch prey. These twilight

Many people believe that cats hate water. This is completely wrong in the case of some species for whom water plays an important, if not essential, part in their lives. Even tigers and jaguars sometimes hunt by waiting in water with just the top of their heads showing. When their prey comes to drink, then the cat attacks. Some, like the fishing cat of southern China, specialize in living in marshes and other wet areas where they catch frogs and fish.

3
Breeding

The best time for a wild animal to give birth is when there is a lot of food around for the babies. In Europe and North America, winters are hard and cold. So the native cats, for instance lynx, bobcats and wildcats, have their young in spring to give the youngsters plenty of time to eat and grow strong before the onset of winter when food is harder to find. In the tropics the problems are slightly different. In the same way that cats of more temperate regions avoid breeding in winter, cats of the tropics avoid giving birth during the wet season when it rains for days on end, making hunting difficult. They usually give birth during the dry season when life is a little easier. But some small African cats, the serval for example, seem to breed in any season, and will have up to three *litters* in a year.

Male and female cats keep well away from each other most of the time, only coming together to mate. Small cats will find each other and mate in just a few hours. Afterward they will go their

From birth, this young cheetah (above) has claws that are always fully extended, just like its mother's. Lion cubs (right) are nosy animals and will thoroughly investigate anything new.

separate ways and might never see each other again. The bigger species take things much more slowly. Tigers will stay together for up to two weeks during the mating season. But, in the end, the male always leaves the female to rear the cubs alone.

Cats like to give birth in quiet, safe places: bobcats choose hollow logs; leopards prefer caves; lions, jaguars and cheetahs seek out areas of thick undergrowth with a sufficient cover of long grass or shrubs.

When cubs are born they are blind and completely helpless. At birth, tiger cubs weigh about two pounds but, like all cat offspring, they grow very quickly, living on their mother's milk for the first few weeks of life. Their teeth start to

Tiger cubs stay with their parents until about their second year, by which time they are almost fully grown.

appear after about fourteen days, and their eyes open when they are five or six weeks old. Then the hard work begins for the mother. Young cubs start exploring as soon as they can see. They spend hours play-fighting, learning how to stalk, pounce, and catch prey. But instead of creeping up on zebra or gazelles, baby lions ambush their brothers and sisters or even leaves blowing in the breeze. This is an important learning stage before they actually go out with their mother to hunt. Cheetah females teach their cubs to hunt by letting them catch the smaller animals and learn by their mistakes. Leopard cubs follow close behind their mother, copying her every movement until they are as skillful as she. As the cubs get older they start to catch their own food, and slowly the bond between the mother and her cubs diminishes. Lynx cubs stay with their mother for only nine months, jaguars for two years and tigers for about two years. Eventually the female stops feeding the youngsters completely and they wander off to find their own territory.

4
Hunting

Cats are *carnivores*, or meateaters. In order to survive, they have to catch and kill other animals. What they catch depends on the size of the cat. Lions, working in a team, can pull down a wildebeeste the size of a horse. But the tiny Geoffroys cat keeps to more manageable birds and small mammals.

Although cats can move very fast, they cannot maintain high speeds for long. In fact, they do not really chase their prey, they ambush it. When a cat first sees a possible prey animal, it crouches low to the ground with ears flattened and head low. For some reason, crouching cats often twitch their tails backwards and forwards, but no one really knows why.

The next stage is for the cat to check the wind direction. Prey species use their noses just as much as predators. They sniff the air every few minutes, checking for dangerous scents. The cats know this, and always try to approach from downwind; in this way their telltale smell is blown right away from their target. When a cat stalks, its movements are almost unnaturally slow: each step seems to take minutes. A *stalking* cat puts the edge of its paw onto the ground first and then lowers its full weight. This cuts down the noise. A hunting lion might weigh up to 550 pounds, but it makes no more sound than a kitten.

The point of stalking, and of using any natural cover for concealment, is to take the cat as close as possible to its prey. It is surprisingly hard to

All cats will hunt for small prey if they are hungry, but it takes many mice to provide a good meal for a bobcat.

Tigers will stay close to their kill and will eat from it until only the bones remain.

see a completely motionless leopard lying in grass, even when it is only a few feet away. The final – and most difficult – part of the hunt is the sprint. If the cat is skillful at stalking, its prey is taken by surprise. But prey animals have learned to be observant and quick, and most attacks end in failure. Familiar, small, mice-eating cats will probably kill once in three or four attempts, but larger species – the tigers, for example, that hunt the agile and graceful axis deer – might kill only once in seven or eight attempts. Small animals are usually quickly killed by a swift and sure bite. Larger ones are, of course, harder to dispatch. Lions and tigers usually kill their large prey by biting hard into the animal's neck and suffocating it.

Some cats are specialist hunters, using their own peculiar techniques. A curious example is the caracal lynx from Africa and Asia, one of the quickest cats in the world. It hunts birds, but doesn't wait for them to land on the ground. Caracals leap high into the air and catch the birds as they fly overhead.

Small cats, such as this margay (above) of Central America, often take food into the treetops to stop it from being stolen by larger predators. Right: a cheetah and its topi prey, which it has killed by suffocation.

5
Cats at Night

Lions (top) are at their most active at night, making this the best time to study their behavior. Above: a black-footed cat.

There are many reasons why most cats have evolved to hunt at night. In the tropics it is cooler at night, and movement, especially rapid movement, is less of an effort than it would be during the heat of the day. Besides, mice, rats and rabbits – common prey animals – are most active at night; during the day they hide away in runs and burrows. On the other hand, animals that normally sleep at night are easier to catch. Deer, antelope and other daytime animals are not well-equipped to see in total darkness. This gives another advantage to a hunting cat.

Cats can see particularly well at night because their eyes have developed a tapetum, a special reflecting membranous layer of cells which surrounds the light-receptor layer of the eye. The tapetum acts just like a mirror, reflecting back all available light onto the receptor layer. It shows up clearly, glowing red or green, when a light is shone into a cat's eyes at night. The cat's iris also opens wide at night, letting in all available light, and closes up to form the characteristic slit in bright light.

However, good eyes alone are not enough to catch prey. The smallest of all cats is the delicate, black-footed cat of southern Africa. It is completely nocturnal and, as it hunts, it stops every few minutes to listen. Cats' ears are very sensitive and can pick up the tiniest sound. The ears of the black-footed cat, like those of all other cat species, act as little radar dishes. They can move independently of each other, picking up sounds in front of them, then to the side. Even the slightest rustle of leaves is enough to give away the presence of a scurrying mouse. This combination of night sight and keen hearing helps the hunting cat pinpoint its prey so efficiently.

When people see lions for the first time it is usually in daylight, and under the hot African sun they seem to be supremely lazy animals. They lie about under trees, sleeping and *grooming*. However, most of the action in a lion's life takes place under the cover of darkness. Kills in progress are hardly ever seen, the only visible evidence of them is the sight of the pride in the morning eating the zebra or wildebeeste caught during the night.

In darkness, the animal world is less noisy: birds are silent, and fewer animals move about. The ability to move about soundlessly is therefore vital to a cat for hunting success in the still, silent night.

A lioness and her cubs with a recently-killed kudu. The tapetum at the back of the cat's eye reflects the light of the photographer's flash.

6
Cats and Man

Before cave-dwelling man invented weapons of stone or metal, big cats were one of his most dangerous enemies. Cats were far more common and widespread then than they are now. Some 15,000 years ago, lions roamed Europe. Now such an exotic sight is almost unthinkable. The silent, nocturnal lynx, for example, once indigenous, became *extinct* in the British Isles around 1,500 years ago. Some of the cats disappeared because the weather in Europe became colder; lions in particular do not like low temperatures. Others, such as the wildcat, were driven out of England because the forests they lived in were cut down. But the biggest threat to the cats was man and his weapons.

Until recently man had a strange relationship with cats. He liked having small cats nearby because they kept down the numbers of rats and mice. He even tamed the North African hunting cat and kept it as a pet. But early man's relationship with big cats was different. Although he respected them for their power and speed and admired the beauty of their coats, they were big and dangerous, and so he feared and destroyed them. The invention of gunpowder and rifles has probably caused the extinction of some species and certainly *endangered* many more. The Bengal tiger in particular has had a very unhappy time. At the beginning of the twentieth century there were around 60,000 wild tigers in Asia; now there are only around 4,000. Over-hunting by man caused most of the tigers' survival problems. People once believed that there was an endless supply of these animals; one famous hunter alone killed 1,150 during his lifetime. Fortunately it is now widely understood that tigers are in danger of extinction and most shooting is now done with a camera instead of a gun.

One of the excuses most often given for killing big cats is that they attack humans. However, over the past 500 years cats have learned to be very wary of humans. Despite their size, they are no match for a high-powered rifle.

Cats are just as frightened of us as we are of them. But it has to be said that occasionally a man-eater does appear. Lions, leopards and tigers have all been known to prey on humans. The culprits are usually old or injured animals that are too slow or clumsy to catch their usual food. Once a cat has killed a human, it discovers that, without weapons, man cannot harm it and, disarmed, is much easier to catch than deer or gazelles. Even *conservationists* agree that man-eaters are just too dangerous to have around. But stories of man-eaters are much more common than the actual animals. Very few big cats ever attack humans; they would rather keep well away from us.

In Britain the European wildcat (above) lives only in the more remote parts of Scotland, having been wiped out in other areas. Varying greatly in both color and size, the domestic cat (facing page) is the most common species of cat.

7
Big Cats of the Forest

Big cats are well designed for life in tropical jungles. Their *camouflage*, climbing skills and ability to move silently through undergrowth make them the most dangerous of woodland hunters.

Tigers are the biggest cats in the world and they are mainly seen in the forests of Asia. Once there were eight subspecies of tiger, each different in size and color, now there may be only five left – no one knows exactly as wild tigers are difficult to study. The Indian tiger, with its bright orange coat and black stripes, is the most common subspecies. But the largest is the Siberian tiger, which can weigh up to 850 pounds and reach thirteen feet in length. This huge cat lives on the border between Russia and China, where the winter temperature can fall as low as -30°F. To keep out the bitter cold, the Siberian tiger has much thicker fur than the other cats. All tigers normally have darker stripes, even the rare white tigers of northern India – only one pure white

tiger has ever been recorded. These stripes help to camouflage tigers, enabling them to stalk unobserved in long grass or to lie in the dappled sunlight under trees waiting for prey.

In the same way that tigers have stripes to conceal them from their prey, jaguars – the big cats of South America – have spots as camouflage. Jaguars are the third largest species of cat and they make their home in dense woodlands and swamps. They can swim and climb very well but do most of their hunting on the ground. They are short, broad and very strongly built, capable of killing monkeys, deer and even cattle. They often bury any spare food they cannot eat, to be dug up and eaten at a later date. This is unusual behavior for a cat, and jaguars do other strange things besides: sometimes, for instance, they suddenly leave their home territory and wander off. They have been known to travel distances of up to 500 miles, but no one knows why they do it.

Leopards seem to feel most at home in woodland, but they can survive in deserts, mountains and even in some built-up areas.

The tiger's markings provide it with perfect camouflage as it stalks through the thick forest undergrowth.

The jaguar (above) is the only true big cat living on the American continent. It is similar to a leopard, but is heavier and stronger. Many local experts believe that the leopard (right) is the most dangerous animal to man in Africa.

Furthermore, unlike other big cats, they do not roar. They only cough, snarl and grunt.

The most widespread of the big cats are the leopards. They are not quite as big as jaguars but are stockier than cheetahs, and they live in Africa and Asia over a wide range of *environments*, from forest to savannah. Like all spotted cats, no two leopards have the same pattern on their coats so none of the cats look exactly alike. But there is one kind that looks very different from the others. Black panthers were once thought to be a distinct species, but in fact they are black-coated leopards.

8
Big Cats of the Open Spaces

Africa is home to some of the most spectacular cats in the world, and the most famous of these must be the lion. For many people these huge cats really are "kings of the jungle," but in fact lions rarely go into woods. They like to live in the vast open spaces of the savannah or grassland, where their golden-brown coats provide perfect camouflage for hunting in long grass.

A lion's life is centred around its pride: a family group of up to thirty cats. Each pride is ruled by a large adult male who keeps his position for only a couple of years. The strain of defending the pride against possible enemies and rival lions soon wears him out and, eventually, he is challenged and succeeded by a younger male.

This lioness has brought down a gnu which is much bigger and heavier than herself.

Most of the hunting is done by the lionesses of the pride; the females are much faster and more agile than the heavier males. Once a kill has been made, all the lions in the pride join in the feast.

Male lions may have to fight viciously for the right to lead a pride. To protect them against the teeth and claws of rivals, the male lion has a thick mat of hair around its neck. This familiar mane makes the male lion look even larger, and a male with a very thick, shaggy mane can sometimes take over a pride with relatively little fighting, simply because he looks so powerful.

Lions are not the only cats that stalk the African plains; they share the *habitat* with cheetahs. Few cheetahs now remain in southern Asia and the Middle East, areas where the lion was also commonly to be found until early this century. Although cheetahs are not as powerful or as heavy as lions, their long, strong legs make them the fastest mammal on earth. When running at full speed, a cheetah can move at a speed of over sixty miles an hour. But if the chase lasts

Superbly adapted for speed, the cheetah (above) is one of the fastest animals on earth. However, the cheetah can only maintain its top speed over a very limited distance. Facing page: a lion drinking at a pool. During the dry season, most cats stay close to water as they need to drink regularly to survive.

much longer than sixty seconds at this sort of speed, the cheetah becomes rapidly exhausted and has to stop. These cats are perfectly designed for short, high-speed sprints, however: they have small heads to keep down their weight; their backs are long and flexible to give them an incredibly long stride, and their tails are used to maintain their balance when they change direction at speed. Cheetahs also have specialized feet, differing from those of any other cat in that their claws are always fully stretched out. During a chase, these long, sharp claws grip the ground, boosting the cat's acceleration.

9
Big Cats of the Wilderness Areas

The mountains of Asia are home to the snow leopard, perhaps the most mysterious and elusive of all the big cats. The remoteness of their habitat and their shy, secretive behavior makes these cats incredibly difficult to study. The beautiful snow leopard of the Himalayas and Hindu Kush is probably the rarest and least understood of all the big cats. They are a highly endangered species, with possibly only a few hundred left in the wild. Unfortunately, herdsmen have been killing snow leopards for centuries to protect their flocks of sheep and goats – they had every need to worry, snow leopards are one of the fastest and most agile hunters known to man.

Snow leopards live at much higher *altitudes* than any other cat. Much of their life is spent high above the snow line. Here the air is so cold that the snow and ice never melt, even in summer. Accordingly, the snow leopard's coat is long and thick with a woolly underlining. The soles of their feet are furred for warmth and to help them friction-grip the surface of the slippery snow and ice. The slopes of the Himalayas are steep and rocky, laced with chasms and ravines which make fast movement difficult and dangerous. To draw near to their prey, snow leopards stalk them as closely as possible, in just the same way as other cats, but the catch itself is usually made by means of a spectacular leap: snow leopards have been seen to jump up to fifty feet in a single bound. These cats will prey on anything, from marmots and goats to wild pigs.

In the dense forests of Asia lives another species that is just as elusive as the snow leopard. Clouded leopards are the smallest of the big cats, weighing only up to forty-five pounds. They are solid, heavily built cats with short legs and a

The clouded leopard is a tree-dweller that lives mainly on small mammals and birds.

The clouded leopard (above), the smallest of the big cats, is named for the relatively large dark patches on its light coat. The snow leopard (left) lives at higher altitudes than other cats. Relatively little is known about these shy and increasingly rare animals.

long tail. Their bodies have evolved to be well-suited to life in trees. They can even travel upside down along branches, clinging on with their claws, and have also been seen hanging onto branches with just one back paw before dropping onto prey below. They can run down trees headfirst, something that no other cat can do, and hunt for monkeys or birds high up in the *forest canopy*, rarely venturing onto the floor where their short legs, so useful in the trees, make them slow and clumsy. Because of the twilight life they live tucked away in dense, and often not easily accessible, tropical forests, very little is known about clouded leopards.

10
Small Mountain Cats

The silent and secretive cougar (above and facing page) inhabits both North and South America, its habitats including mountain, desert and sub-Arctic terrain. At just twelve months old the young cougar is strong enough to kill a fully grown deer.

Mountains are often cold, uninviting areas where survival is a struggle. The little-known Chinese desert cat lives in the high Asian mountains, where summers are roasting hot and winter temperatures fall well below zero. Like other mountain-dwelling cats, this one, which is the size of a domestic cat, has fur on the bottom of its feet. High up in the same Asian mountains there is another cat that has to cope with some of the worst weather conditions on earth: the Pallas cat hunts in remote wilderness regions where there are no trees and even grass is rare. In winter the cold there is terrible and, to cope with it, the build of the Pallas cat has become specialized. It has very short legs and short ears in order to cut down heat loss and prevent frostbite, and its longest hair is on its underside to keep it warm when it is walking through snow.

The best known of all mountain cats is the puma. In its native countries of Canada and the United States it is sometimes called the cougar or mountain lion. Pumas are the biggest of the "small" cats, sometimes over eight feet long and 220 pounds in weight. They are most at home in the Rocky Mountains, where deer and antelope are still common and supply most of the puma's diet. These cats are known as the "ghosts of North America" because they are so silent and secretive. Usually the only way to tell if a puma has been near is to look out for the footprints. Few animals in the world can match the puma's skill at hunting without being seen, even in broad daylight.

11
Small Forest Cats

Small cats belong in woodland. Everything about them – their stealth, climbing ability and leaping skills – is perfectly designed for forest life. Three quarters of the world's small cats live in and around trees. But, as in the case of the clouded leopard, this often means that they remain hidden from human eyes. We still know very little about the lives of many forest cats.

For example, few people have studied the strange, flat-headed cat of Borneo and Sumatra. In addition to its oddly shaped head, the cat is unusual because it cannot fully retract its claws. The South American jaguarundi is an equally

Although it inhabits dense jungle, the golden cat usually stays on the ground.

peculiar cat that inhabits woodlands. Its body is long and low and its head is small and pointed, making it look more like a mongoose. The locals call it eyra (in its reddish brown form) or otter-cat because of its odd appearance and swimming ability. Although the jaguarundi lives around trees, it stays mainly on the ground, hunting rabbits and mice. They only scale trees as a last resort if they are attacked by bigger animals.

The beautiful Asian and African golden cats can be described as true jungle animals. The ferocity of these animals is well-documented by locals. They say that golden cats can kill animals more than twice their size. Out of respect for its strength they call it the "leopard cat." There is also a real leopard cat in the forests of Asia; it looks like a miniature version of its bigger

The jaguarundi of Central and South America hunts mainly at dusk, feeding on a variety of prey and also occasionally eating fruit.

namesake. These cats are still common and their numbers are relatively unaffected by man. Indeed, unusually enough, the leopard cat is often found close to villages. It has learned that there are large numbers of rats and mice around wherever humans store their food and throw away their rubbish. Small villages at night are, therefore, rich hunting grounds.

A thousand years ago, wildcats could be found all over Britain, throughout Europe, and all the way to India. They look a little like tabby cats, having heavy, long legs and thick, ringed tails. Wildcats are powerful and very fast animals, and they prey on small mammals and birds. In Britain, until the nineteenth century, there was a government reward for anyone who killed a wildcat. Thousands were destroyed; consequently they can now only be found in the forests and moors of Scotland, and are one of the most wary and cautious of all cats. They are totally nocturnal and stay well away from man. In most places wildcats are legally protected, but hunting still goes on nonetheless. Apart from the activities of man, the fact that wildcats breed easily with domestic cats is one of the biggest threats to its remaining a distinct species.

12
Small Cats of the Open Spaces

At first glance, deserts would not appear to the best habitats for cats. The extreme heat, scarcity of water and poor availability of prey animals are just some of the problems a desert-dwelling predator must face. But there are also some advantages for animals that move into harsh and difficult habitats. For a start, there is little competition for food. In tropical forests there are many hunting animals, all looking for prey and, therefore, competing with each other for available food.

In true deserts water is scarce; it can sometimes be as long as three or four years between rainstorms. Accordingly, the wildlife that lives in such regions has to adapt to long periods without water. The best adapted and most skilful desert cat is the caracal, or desert lynx, from Africa and Asia. Their huge eyes, smooth coats and long, tasselled ears also make caracals one of the most beautiful cats. The caracal lynx probably drinks less than any other cat, gaining most of the moisture it needs from the bodies of its prey and, to escape the scorching daytime heat, it hunts at night and will chase almost anything that moves; it even hunts venomous snakes. Although the poison of cobras

During the cold winter months, bobcats (above) grow extra-long fur as protection against the severe cold. Found in parts of Africa and India, the caracal (facing page) is perhaps the best adapted desert cat. In India these cats were once trained to catch rabbits and birds for humans to eat.

and puff adders could easily kill it, the caracal's attack is so fast that the snakes just do not have time to strike.

The North American bobcat, smallest of the American cats, is also at home in wide open spaces. The animal gets its name from its stubby tail, which makes it look like a small lynx. The bobcat's diet consists mainly of rabbits and hares, which it chases and knocks over with its very large front paws. Weak or injured bobcats are themselves sometimes killed and eaten by the bigger lynx and puma.

The huge areas of open grassland, called savanna in Africa and pampas in South America, provide rich hunting grounds for small cats, such as the serval of southern Africa. These wary animals are the size of domestic cats and have big, rounded ears that give them very acute hearing. They live off birds, rodents and reptiles, and when they get really hungry servals, like all cats, will even eat insects. The South American version of the serval is called the pampas cat. However, this cat is much less common than the serval because every year thousands of acres of its pampas habitat is turned into farmland.

The long-limbed serval is an inhabitant of southern Africa, living off birds, rodents and reptiles.

13
Cats in Danger

Of the thirty-five species of cat in the world, fifteen are under some threat of extinction. Over-hunting is still a problem, and even in these days of well-meaning conservation small cats are killed in huge numbers for their skin: each year, for example, around 20,000 Geoffroys cats are destroyed. These delicate animals are already rare and the fur trade is pushing them even closer to the point of extinction. The spotted cats have always been prime targets for fur hunters. The ocelot from North America and the margay from South America, to cite just two examples, are both under pressure from poachers who can easily sell the pelts to fur traders that do not mind breaking the law. Hunting for cat skins is actually controlled by international agreement. Only a certain number can be handled in a year and it is illegal to sell them without permission. But smuggling still goes on regardless all over the world, and many more cats are being killed than the law officially allows.

However, the biggest danger to some cats is not being hunted so much as the destruction of their habitat. The safest animals are those that live in places that humans do not want. The desert cat from China is an example; it lives in dry, rocky land where little grows. Because no one wants to build houses or plant crops there, the cats are left in peace. The same cannot be said about the cats that inhabit forests. Every day, all over the world, vast areas are cut down to produce timber. Once the trees are gone the land is normally used for crops. As the trees are felled the animals have to find somewhere else to live. But if the destruction continues there will be no remaining refuge. The clouded leopard, the elegant tiger cat and the little-known mountain cat are all threatened by this loss of habitat.

There are plenty of difficulties facing wild cats but the future is not all gloomy. Many people are now more interested in conserving

In some countries endangered animals, such as this jaguar, are moved to new areas if their habitat is threatened.

Until recently, the ocelot was often kept as a pet and many females were killed while defending their young from animal catchers.

Resembling the ocelot, the beautiful, sleek margay (above) is a nocturnal inhabitant of Central and South American forests. Cheetahs (right) like sitting on termite hills or rocks so that they can see clearly all around.

animals than in killing them. Organizations like the Worldwide Fund for Nature have set up plans to make sure that endangered animals survive well into the future. Operation Tiger is a good example. With the co-operation of the Indian Government and money donated by the public, new tiger reserves have been created. Here the cats are safe, hunting is illegal and no one can cut down a single tree. With help, all the cats of the world can be protected in similar ways, and surely it is worth a little effort to save some of the most beautiful and exciting animals on earth.

Glossary

ALTITUDE – the height of land above sea level.

CANINE (teeth) – long, sharp teeth, two on the top and two on the bottom jaws, which are used for killing and tearing meat.

CAMOUFLAGE – colored fur or skin that helps an animal to remain hidden in its environment.

CARNIVORE – an animal that kills and eats other animals.

CONSERVATION – the care of plants, animals and natural habitats, to make sure that they can survive into the future.

ENDANGERED SPECIES – a species that is becoming rare and might one day completely die out.

ENVIRONMENT – an animal's surroundings; not only the land but also weather and temperature.

EXTINCT – a species that has died out everywhere in the world eg. dinosaurs.

FOREST CANOPY – the top of the trees, where most of the leaves grow, it is sometimes called the roof of the forest.

GROOMING – licking and scratching fur to keep it clean and unmatted.

HABITAT – the natural home of an animal.

LITTER – a family of newly born animals.

NOCTURNAL – an animal that is active at night and sleeps during the day.

PREY – an animal, or animals, that are killed and eaten by another animal.

SPECIES – a group of animals that can breed with others of their own kind, but not with any other animal.

SCENT GLAND – a part of an animal's body that produces a strong smelling liquid which is used to signal to other animals.

STALKING – slow, silent movements that are used for creeping up close to prey animals.

TERRITORY – an area of land that is home to one animal, from which any other animal of its own species is excluded.

Picture Credits

Anthony Bannister 8, 21, 29; Stanley Breedon 6 *right*; Judd Cooney 24; Michael Dick/ANIMALS ANIMALS 1, 22, 23 *top and bottom*; Carol Farneti/Partridge Films Ltd. 14 *bottom*; Mickey Gibson/ANIMALS ANIMALS 30 *right*; Breck P. Kent/ ANIMALS ANIMALS 25; Tom Leach 28 *bottom*; Colin Milkins 17 *top*; Terry G. Murphy/ANIMALS ANIMALS 20 *right*; John E. Nees/ANIMALS ANIMALS 19 *bottom*; Stan Osolinski 5, 9, 13, 31 *bottom*; Peter O'Toole 17 *bottom*; A. Petretti/Panda Photo 18 *left*; Press-Tige Pictures 16; Partridge Films Ltd. 12, 31 *top*; Partridge Productions Ltd. 27, 30 *left*; Leonard Lee Rue III/ANIMALS ANIMALS 28 *top*; Rafi Ben-Shahar 14 *top*, 15, 20 *left*; Stouffer Enterprises Inc./ANIMALS ANIMALS 11 *left*, 26; Tom Ulrich 6 *left*, 7; Belinda Wright 2, 4, 10, 11 *right*, 18 *right*; Claudia Wight/Partridge Productions Ltd. 19 *top*.